FULLY ALIVE

FULLY ALIVE

THERE IS MORE...

JAMIE MILLER

Consumed Publishing

Consumed Publishing
An extension of Consumed Ministries.
Bloomington MN, 55420
www.consumedministries.com

Consumed Ministries is a message centered ministry that exists to
share the message of abundant, overflowing, more than you can
begin to imagine life found only in knowing God in a deep, intimate and relational way.

Edited by Stephanie Frusher
Design and layout by Eric Beavers

Published in Minneapolis, MN by Consumed Publishing.
Printed by Bethany Press International
6820 W. 115th Street
Bloomington MN, 55348

ISBN 0-9766555-0-0

Library of Congress Control Number: 200690113

Printed in the United States of America.

DEDICATED TO

My two beautiful daughters, Tori & Isabelle. I fight for you. May you always walk in intimacy with Jesus, finding complete and perfect satisfaction in Him alone. I love you as high as the stars!

ACKNOWLEDGMENTS

Words can't express my thanks to you Gretchen. You are an amazing gift from God and my companion and witness on this journey of life. Your love for God and others inspires me to live life to the fullest.

To those God used to point me to life... Mom and Dad — you brought me up in the way of Jesus. Polly — you introduced me to my Savior. Penny and Katie — your prayers and time shaped me into the man I am. Dr. King, Cliff, and Dan — God used you to unplug me from the matrix. I am fully alive because of you.

To everyone involved with Consumed — Eric — your tireless work on this project is only known by God. Mom — thanks for the ideas and proofreading. Stephanie — how did we find you?

To the many others whose lives God intersected with mine — the saints at Immanuel, CrossRoads, BBC, and Alumni Office. There are no coincidences with God.

Lastly and most loudly, I shout out praise and thanksgiving to the giver of life alone... my wonderful Jesus. Your body was torn in two so I could enter the Most Holy Place. Eternity is not long enough for me to worship You! I love you and the Father with all that I am!

CONTENTS

THERE IS MORE

I remember when my world changed as I stood in the middle of North Point Community Church in Alpharetta, GA. I was attending a "Thirsty Conference" for college leaders and campus pastors that was put on by Passion Ministries in the spring of 2002. The worship leader had led us to the throne of God, and we were all expressing heartfelt praise for The King of the Universe. As I observed those in the auditorium, I was moved by what I saw. All around me were children of God singing as loudly as they possibly could, their hands raised toward heaven. Faces radiated the joy of the Lord. A mom and a dad had their two little girls on their shoulders, and the little girls were singing and bouncing, their faces reflecting the freedom they felt. Other worshippers sat in chairs with tears streaming down their faces, obviously moved by their love for Christ. I had never before experienced such an intense and moving time of worship.

In that moment, as the music blared and the lights moved, I realized for the first time that I was missing something in my religious experience. Not something tangible from that moment such as the style of music, the building, or the lights but something beyond the physical realm. Something that was in my own personal spiritual journey. I just knew the Holy Spirit was convincing me there was more. Christianity was so much more than I had known so far.

I thought I had it all. I grew up in a Bible-believing, Jesus-exalting church. I accepted Jesus Christ into my life as my Savior at an early age and was baptized. In high school, I was involved in my youth group. I graduated from Bible college and was taking Seminary classes at the time I attended the conference. I was also a co-leader of the college and singles ministry at my church, and I read my Bible and prayed regularly. Isn't that what Christianity is all about? For the first 22 years of my Christian experience, I had been convinced that those things were all there was. But in that one moment in the spring of 2002, I knew there was more. I didn't know what the more was, but I knew the people around me had it and that I wanted it badly. This pursuit of more led me to the greatest truth found in Scripture. It is a truth that completely changed my life! It is a truth I have committed my life to sharing with anyone that comes across my path. It is the truth I want to share with you in the pages of this book. There really is more...

I.
YOU HAVE LIFE

"I tell you the truth, the man who does not enter the sheep pen by the gate, but climbs in by some other way, is a thief and a robber. The man who enters by the gate is the shepherd of his sheep. The watchman opens the gate for him, and the sheep listen to his voice. He calls his own sheep by name and leads them out. When he has brought out all of his own, he goes on ahead of them, and his sheep follow him because they know his voice. But they will never follow a stranger; in fact, they will run away from him because they do not recognize a stranger's voice."

– John 10:1-5

Now many of you reading this may be like me. If so, you are thinking, "What in the world is Jesus talking about?" You see, I was born and raised in Columbus, OH, and farming is not my scene. I have never milked a cow, shoveled manure, or built a wooden fence. Mix in the fact that Jesus is talking about the way shepherding was done over 2000 years ago in Israel, and I become even more perplexed about His statements.

Let me try and remove some of the haziness. What Jesus is describing is a morning shepherding scene. At that time, many flocks would stay in one sheep pen over night for protection. The sheep pen was built with stonewalls, and a gatekeeper protected the sheep from wild animals and thieves. Many times, there would be an opening without a door. The gatekeeper or watchman would lie down across the entrance of the sheep pen and literally make himself the "door" or "gate" to the sheep pen.

Every morning the various shepherds would come to the sheep pen, enter through the gate, and call out their sheep by name. "Here Sheepy." "Here Freddy." "Rory." Hearing their name, the sheep would leave the sheep pen and follow their shepherd out to the pasture to do whatever it is sheep do all day. Give them credit, sheep are smarter than we think.

They know their shepherd's voice and will not go with anyone except their shepherd. That's why Jesus said that anyone who does not enter through the gate is a thief and a robber. Thieves would climb over the wall and carry the sheep out because it was the only way they could transport the sheep out of the sheep pen. The gate was protected.

> *"Jesus used this figure of speech, but they (he was speaking to Pharisees at the time) did not understand what he was telling them."* **—John 10:6**

These Pharisees were either born and raised in the city of Columbus, OH, like me and did not understand sheep pens or gate keepers, or they were unable to see the spiritual parallel Jesus was trying to communicate, so Jesus went on to explain:

> *"I tell you the truth. I am the gate for the sheep. All who ever came before me were thieves and robbers, but the sheep did not listen to them. I am the gate; whoever enters through me will be saved. He will come in and go out, and find pasture. The thief comes only to steal and kill and destroy…"* **—John 10:7-10a**

What a wonderful picture! Jesus tells them, "I am literally the gate. I lie down at the entrance of the sheep pen and protect the sheep from thieves and robbers." We will not get into this now, but Jesus, in an indirect way, accuses the Pharisees of being thieves and robbers (check out John 9). Any sheep that enters the pen through Jesus, "The Gate," will be saved. They will come in and out of the sheep pen and find enjoyment and fulfillment in the pasture.

The thief Jesus referred to in verse 10 is Satan himself. He is the enemy of God, and the enemy of God's image bearers. Satan's purpose statement was very clear. He exists to "kill, steal, and destroy" the Gatekeeper's sheep. He is hell-bent on climbing over the wall of the sheep pen to destroy the lives of the sheep. He is the "roaring lion, looking for someone to devour." I am glad for the ultimate Gatekeeper who promised safety, enjoyment, satisfaction, and love. Satan is powerless against Him.

Well, I left out one final phrase in these first ten verses ... the phrase that changed my life ... the phrase I pray from the innermost part of my soul will change your life as well. Jesus says in verse 10, *"The thief comes only to steal and kill and destroy...*

But I have come that they (sheep) **may have life***, and have it to the* **full***."*   *–John 10:10*

Wow, simply amazing. Are you kidding me? The Son of the Most High God left His throne in heaven to dwell among men for the purpose of giving us **life**. And not just any life, I mean life is good enough. Because of my sin, I was "dead in my transgressions in sins, in which I used to live when I followed the ways of this world and of the ruler of the kingdom of the air..." There was no hope for me. I was an "object of God's wrath." But through faith in Christ, I was "made alive." I am free of sin and am confident of my citizenship in heaven. Believe me that is good enough. That is incredible news. Yet Jesus takes it one step further when He says, *"I have come that they may have life..."* but not just life, "life to the **full**." Literally, life "abundantly," life "overflowing," or life "exceedingly abundant." As one commentator (what commentator?) put it, "More than one would normally expect or anticipate." We have overflowing, exceedingly abundant, more than we can begin to imagine, expect, or conceive kind of life. That is why Jesus came. That's what He wants to give His "sheep." Pause a moment...revel in this amazing truth!

That is the reason for this book. My desire and prayer is that after reading it you will understand in your mind and in your heart one thing—**you have life**. Christ came for you to experience this amazing, abundant life. If you have accepted the gift of grace from God through faith, **you have life**. As a matter of fact, this may seem silly but, if it's true say to yourself right now, out loud: "Self, I have life." Now, I know many of you are like me, cynical and not prone to follow instructions like this from an author, but this time really say it—"I have life!" Say it one more time to truly commit yourself to believing this truth of Scripture, which is written in the red ink of Jesus' own words: "I have life!"

If you still are having a tough time believing me or accepting this because abundant life is not what you have either perceived or experienced yourself or in the lives of other Christians in your local fellowship, let the Scriptures saturate your thinking by reading what Christ said at other times in the book of John…

*"…that everyone who believes in him may have eternal **life**" (3:15).*

*"…that whoever believes in him shall not perish, but have everlasting **life**" (3:16).*

*"…but whoever drinks the water I give him will never thirst. Indeed, the water I give him will become in him a spring of water welling up to eternal **life**" (4:14).*

*"For just as the Father raises the dead and gives them **life**, even so the Son gives **life**…" (5:21).*

*"...whoever hears my word and believes him who sent me has eternal **life**...he has crossed over from death to **life**" (5:24).*

*"For the bread of God is he who comes down from heaven and gives **life** to the world" (6:33).*

*"I am the bread of **life**" (6:35).*

*"For my Father's will is that everyone who looks to the Son and believes in him shall have eternal **life**..." (6:40).*

*"I am the resurrection and the **life**" (11:25).*

*"I am the way, the truth, and the **life**" (14:6).*

*"...and that by believing you may have **life** in his (Jesus) name" (20:31).*

Are you starting to buy in? I just wrote for you a small portion of the book of John. John mentions "life" 33 times in his book alone. I didn't even begin to touch on the countless times throughout the rest of the Bible where "life" is the topic being discussed. Passages in the Old Testament like Psalm 16:11 when it says:

*"You have made know to me the path of **life**."* Or in the New Testament like Romans 6:23, *"...but the gift of God is eternal **life**."* It's everywhere—cover to cover. You can't escape this major thread of the Bible. God desires for us to have overflowing, abundant, eternal, **life**!

We need to clarify the meaning of "eternal life." Often, we rob the true meaning by limiting it to simply our future home in heaven. We believe eternal life begins in one of two places—Christ's return or our death. Again, eternal life would be good enough. If this were the only offer on the table, I would accept it quickly. But we definitely were not meant to have abundant, eternal life here on earth, right? I mean we just need to toil on, "endure our hardships like a good soldier," try not to sin, realize this life stinks, and cognizant one day it will be worth it all. Amen, brother! Well, actually that is dead wrong. I do not agree with that logic one bit and feel it is a travesty. It robs Christ of what He came to accomplish for us. John Eldridge speaks of this in *Waking the Dead* when he writes:

"Jesus doesn't locate his offer to us only in some distant future after we've slogged our way through our days here on earth. He talks about a life available to us in this age. So does Paul: 'Godliness has value for all things, holding promise for both the present life and the life to come' (I Tim. 4:8). Our present life and the next. When we hear the words eternal life, most of us interpret that as 'life that waits for us in eternity.' But eternal means 'unending,' not 'later.' The Scriptures use the term to mean we can never lose it. It's a life that can't be taken from us. The offer is life, and that life starts now."

Does that mean we will not experience trials, temptation, and sufferings? NO! But I do believe we can experience abundant living in the midst of those experiences. At the point of salvation, we have an unending, overflowing, more that you can begin to comprehend or imagine life. That's what I desire. That's what you long for, isn't it? Start believing that is what God desires for you. Jesus Christ is the Source. It's one of the reasons He came. It's the reason He was beaten, spit upon, crushed, bruised, mocked, slapped, and crucified. It's the reason He conquered death and burst forth from the tomb. It's yours! Claim it! Start living it! But how...

II.
LIFE DEFINED

At one point in my life, I was an assistant basketball coach at a NCAA Division III college. Throughout my four-year coaching experience, our staff would attend NIKE Championship Basketball Clinics to receive instruction from big time NCAA Division I and NBA coaches on various aspects of the game. I sat under the tutelage of Dean Smith, Hubie Brown, Tom Izzo, Roy Williams, and Gary Williams to name a few. Our staff would walk away from these clinics excited to implement into our system many of the things we had just learned.

During one of these sessions at a clinic in Cleveland, OH, Coach Dan Monson from the University of Minnesota spoke. He emphasized the importance of everyone on the coaching staff understanding and using the same basketball terminology to avoid confusing the players. He told us a story about one of his first collegiate coaching experiences. At that time, he was a young coach who was close to the age of the players on the team. During one practice, the team was working on a drill, and the head coach continually told the team to "seam it." Coach Monson, however, had no clue what the head coach was talking about when he said "seam it." A couple of the players came to Coach Monson and asked, "What does coach mean by 'seam it'?" Coach Monson, trying to protect his ignorance and keep the respect of his players, responded to the question by stating: "You know what coach means. Seam it. Come on, seam it. Get back to work."

You may laugh at this story, but our Christian vocabulary and clichés are full of their own "seam its." How often do you throw out Christian clichés or terms that you would be hard-pressed to define? I recently asked a community class I was teaching what the word "hallelujah" meant. No one in a group of 35 could give me an answer. We use the word "hallelujah" often in our Christian circles. Some of you are like me and grew up saying and hearing phrases such as "Hallelujah, brother," or "Oh, hallelujah, He answered my prayer." In case you're wondering "hallelujah" comes from the Hebrew word for praise "hallal," which means to be clamorously foolish or mad before the Lord.

If we are not careful, "abundant life" can become one of those Christian expressions or clichés we talk about but really do not understand or know how to define or explain. We can talk a lot about abundant life and the fact that Christ came to give us abundant life, but we don't understand how it affects our daily lives. What does abundant life look like when I'm working, studying, partying, drinking a mocha, playing at a gym, golfing, attending church, driving, etc.?

Know or KNOW?

Once again, let's look to the master teacher to clue us in on this so we'll have an explanation. In John 17, the longest prayer of Jesus is recorded. Jesus is preparing Himself for the horrific events which will soon transpire at His arrest, trial, and execution. In this prayer, He asks His Father to glorify Himself so that Jesus can glorify the Father. He then goes on to pray for His disciples and for all believers (this includes you and me). Early on in the chapter Jesus prays:

> *"Father, the time has come. Glorify your Son, that your Son may glorify you. For you granted him authority over all people that he might give eternal life to those you have given them. Now this is eternal life…"*

At this very moment, your eyebrows should be raised. You should be sitting on the edge of your seat. It is like the end of a football game when your favorite team is down by two points, and the field goal kicker is preparing to do his thing. Or that crucial part in a suspense thriller when the murderer is finally going to be revealed. Did you hear what Jesus said? "Now this is eternal life…" Jesus is going to dial us into what unending, abundant, more than you can begin to comprehend life is.

"Now this is eternal life: that they may know you, the only true God, and Jesus Christ, whom you have sent."

That's it? That's all there is to unending, abundant life? To know God and Jesus? How simple! How elementary! There has to be more. You may be thinking to yourself, "I already know this. I said the prayer when I was five at Vacation Bible School. I go to church, sing in the choir, tithe regularly, read my Bible, and pray. I know God." Do you really?

In the Greek New Testament, there are two words for "know." The first Greek word means to understand, to be acquainted with, and to recognize. The second Greek word means to learn, perceive, to be very certain. It carries the idea of intimacy and depth. It even can even refer to having knowledge of in a sexual way.

You see, I "know" the employees of the local Krispy Kreme. I go there every Saturday with my daughter Tori on our weekly father-daughter date. I am acquainted with them, and they recognize Tori and I when we walk in each Saturday. But I "know" my wife Gretchen in a far different way than I "know" the employees of Krispy Kreme. Do you see the difference?

In John 17, Jesus says eternal life is knowing God. But this word for knowing goes well beyond the idea of being acquainted with or recognizing who God is. This is where I lived for far too long. I served at church, preached sermons, tried to be a godly husband and father, strove to be a faithful and disciplined employee at work, studied my Bible, and prayed. I was acquainted with God. I recognized Him and was familiar with Him. I had enough head knowledge to talk theology with whomever. I earned a Bachelor's degree in Bible and was enrolled in a Master of Divinity program. I knew about God, but I didn't "know" God.

How would you rate your knowledge of God this very moment? Do you "know" God, or do you "know" God? Does your relationship with God impact every area of your life? Or have you compartmentalized Christianity and slotted God into your "Christian activities" such as doing your devotions and going to church? Do you wave to God when you see Him and say, "Hey there's God over there. I'm glad I'm acquainted with Him, and He recognizes me. One day I'll truly spend time with Him in heaven." Or do you sense the presence of God in every area of your life? Do you journey intimately with Him 24/7? Do you know God? Do you truly love Him? Do you have a relationship with Him?

An Amazing Calling

Some of my favorite passages of Scripture show men being given the privilege to see visions of God on His throne. Here are three:

"In the year that King Uzziah died, I saw the LORD seated on a throne, high and exalted, and the train of his robe filled the temple. Above him were seraphs, each with six wings: With two wings they covered their faces, with two they covered their feet, and with two they were flying. And they were calling to one another:

> *'Holy, holy, holy is the Lord Almighty; the whole earth is full of his glory.'*

At the sound of their voices the doorposts and thresholds shook and the temple was filled with smoke."
— Isaiah 6:1-5

"Then there came a voice from above the expanse over their heads as they stood with lowered wings. Above the expanse over their heads was what looked like a throne of sapphire, and high above on the throne was a figure like that of a man. I saw that from what appeared to be his waist up he looked like glowing metal, as if full of fire, and that from there down he looked like fire; and brilliant light surrounded him. Like the appearance of a rainbow in the clouds on a rainy day, so was the radiance around him.

This was the appearance of the likeness of the glory of the LORD. When I saw it, I fell facedown, and I heard the voice of one speaking." – Ezekiel 1:25-28

"At once I was in the Spirit, and there before me was a throne in heaven with someone sitting on it. And the one who sat there had the appearance of jasper and

carnelian. A rainbow, resembling an emerald, encircled the throne. Surrounding the throne were twenty-four other thrones, and seated on them were twenty-four elders. They were dressed in white and had crowns of gold on their heads. From the throne came flashes of lightning, rumblings, and peals of thunder. Before the throne, seven lamps were blazing. These are the seven spirits of God. Also before the throne there was what looked like a sea of glass, clear as crystal.

In the center, around the throne, were four living creatures, and they were covered with eyes, in front and in back. The first living creature was like a lion, the second was like an ox, the third had a face like a man, and the fourth was like a flying eagle. Each of the four living creatures had six wings and was covered with eyes all around, even under his wings. Day and night they never stop saying:

'Holy, holy, holy is the Lord God Almighty, who was, and is, and is to come.'" – Revelation 4:2-8

I get goose bumps every time I read those inspired words. I love the writers' attempts to describe what they are seeing. "It was like this," "they were like that." It reminds me of two middle school students conversing in the hallway between classes. "And he was like"... "and she was like"... "No way."

Ezekiel wrote, "This was the appearance of the likeness of the glory of God." He wasn't struggling to describe the glory of God. He was trying just to paint a picture of the appearance of the likeness of the glory of God.

I mentioned at the beginning of this section that some of my favorite passages of Scripture are men trying desperately to describe with mere words their visions of God. However, there are other passages of Scripture I enjoy even more than those.

"For he chose us in him before the creation of the world to be holy and blameless in his sight. In love he predestined us to be adopted as his sons through Jesus Christ." – *Ephesians 1:4-5*

"But because of his great love for us, God, who is rich in mercy, made us alive with Christ even when we were dead in transgressions – it is by grace you have been saved. And God raised us up with Christ and seated us with him in the heavenly realms with Christ Jesus." – *Ephesians 2:4-6*

"Consequently, you are no longer foreigners and aliens, but fellow citizens with God's people and members of God's household." – *Ephesians 2:19*

"You are all sons of God through faith in Christ Jesus, for all of you who were baptized into Christ have clothed yourselves with Christ." – Galatians 3:26-27

Let these truths sink in! Park it. Settle down right here for awhile and dwell on these words. The God of the Universe, the Creator of the World, I AM, The Most High, The One Ezekiel, Isaiah, and John couldn't adequately describe because of His lofty grandeur has brought you into His family through the blood of His Son. How awesome is that? It completely blows my mind. I can't fully comprehend it. I am simply overwhelmed.

Abundant life is knowing the Creator of the universe as your Father. Romans 8 tells us: "For you did not receive a spirit that makes you a slave again to fear, but you received the Spirit of sonship. And by him we cry, 'Abba, Father'." We have the ability to call the great I AM almost literally "Daddy, Father." That's how deep this relationship goes. That's how amazing abundant life is. We know the Father!

Who are we?

A.W. Tozer once said, "The most important thing you think about, is what you think about, when you think about God." If I may expand on Tozer's statement (Jamie Miller adding to Tozer, scary), the second most important thing you think about is what you think God sees when He looks at you. Have you ever thought about that? Coming to grips with how God views you is vitally important to abundant living defined as knowing the Father. If you think God sees a miserable, rotten, worm-like sinner when He looks at you, then your relationship with God will be dramatically hindered. The constant feelings of guilt and unworthiness will keep you from intimacy with your Father. Quite frankly, that thinking says the blood of Jesus was good enough to get you into heaven, but not nearly good enough to allow victory over sin and belief in your inner man that there is truly "no condemnation for those who are in Christ Jesus" (Romans 8:1).

"But thanks be to God that, though you used to be slaves to sin, you wholeheartedly obeyed the form of teaching to which you were entrusted. You have been set free from sin and have become slaves to righteousness."
— *Romans 6:17-18*

Read that verse again. Slowly!

"But thanks be to God that, though you used to be slaves to sin, you wholeheartedly obeyed the form of teaching to which you were entrusted. You have been set free from sin and have become slaves to righteousness."

You have been set free from sin! You are slaves ... not of sin, but of righteousness! As children of the living God, we are not labeled "sinners" in the New Testament. The term sinner is used in the New Testament to describe unsaved people still in Adam. They are slaves to sin, and their lives are characterized by their bondage to sin. Do we still sin? Yes! We most definitely do. Every single solitary day! It ticks me off when I sin, because by sinning, I choose not to live in the freedom given to me through Christ. I live more like an ex-convict who decides to go back to prison from time to time just to hang out. But that is not who we are. That is not the way God's Word describes us. Our Father does not look at His children and see miserable, worm-like, sinners. He looks at His children and sees "slaves of righteousness."

Here is a just a sampling of what the Word of God calls those that have trusted in Christ: The Called, Ambassadors of Christ, Believers, Brothers, Children, Children of God, Children of Light, Children of the Resurrection, Chosen People, Christians, Faithful Followers, Fellow Citizens, Fellow Soldiers, Fools for Christ, Friends, Heirs, Holy Ones, Holy Priesthood, Loyal Yokefellows, Members of God's Household, People of God, Priests, Prisoners of Christ, Righteous, Righteousness of God, Royal Priesthood, Saints, Servants of Christ, Servants of God, Sons, Sons of God, Sons of the Kingdom, Sons of the Most High, Sons of Your Father, Work of God's Hands, and Worshippers. What a list! That's not even all of them! There are more names given to us. We didn't earn these names. We didn't accomplish any of this. God made it possible through the work of Christ and

His grace in our lives. He made us alive! He chose us! He made us sons and daughters of God! He made us members of God's household! The result of God's actions gives us freedom from the bondage of sin and allows us the amazing ability to pursue intimacy with the Father. We can draw near to God because of our position as His children.

> *"Day after day every priest stands and performs his religious duties; again and again he offers the same sacrifices, which can never take away sins. But when this priest (Jesus) had offered for all time one sacrifice for sins, he sat down at the right hand of God. Since that time he waits for his enemies to be made his footstool, because by one sacrifice he has made perfect forever those who are being made holy.*
>
> *The Holy Spirit also testifies to us about this. First he says:*
>
> *'This is the covenant I will make with them after that time, says the LORD. I will put my laws in their hearts and I will write them on their minds.'*

Then he adds:

'Their sins and lawless acts I will remember no more.

And where these have been forgiven, there is no longer any sacrifice for sin.

Therefore, brothers, since we have confidence to enter the Most Holy Place by the blood of Jesus, by a new and living way opened for us through the curtain, that is, his body, and since we have a great priest over the house of God, let us draw near to God with a sincere heart in full assurance of faith, having our hearts sprinkled to cleanse us from a guilty conscience and having our bodies washed with pure water. Let us hold unswervingly to the hope we profess, for he who promised is faithful." – Hebrews 10:11-23

So from here, because of our confidence to enter the very presence of God, let us learn how to "draw near to God." This is the only source of abundant life.

III.
LIFE... IT TAKES TIME

Ten years ago I experienced a moment that forever changed the rest of my life. It is a moment I will never forget, because in that moment, I gazed upon the most amazing sight my eyes had ever seen. I only thought I knew what beautiful was until that moment. I was looking at a woman that transformed the meaning of words like gorgeous, adorable, and breathtaking. I knew I had never seen anyone or anything quite like her in the first nineteen years of life.

It was the beginning of my sophomore year of college. Because I was involved in student leadership, I had returned a couple of days earlier than the rest of the student body. That first evening there was a break between leadership sessions, and I was in the gymnasium, which was practically my second dorm room, shooting some hoops with another guy on the basketball team. As I looked around the gym to check out the other students, I saw her for the first time. She had on a white t-shirt, blue warm-up pants, and sandals, and her brown hair was up in a ponytail. She had the bluest eyes I had ever seen and when she smiled, two cute, very visible dimples appeared. She had this look about her which was the perfect balance between adorable and completely floor you amazingly beautiful. I stood there and stared for what seemed like an eternity, knowing that I was hopelessly infatuated with someone I had never met.

I did manage to meet her and learn her name, but things didn't work out that academic year as I had hoped and dreamed (many nights in my dorm room), but the next year we began to date. The more I learned about her, the more I wanted to learn. What were her dreams, passions, and goals? What was her family like? Did she have past boyfriends? Lucky for me, she didn't. And the more I learned, the more I wanted to see her and be with her. I honestly believed I could have spent every waking moment of every day with her, and it wouldn't have been enough. There was so much I wanted to learn about her.

I have been getting to know her for nine years now with seven of those years being spent as husband and wife. You know what? I still can't get enough of her. There still isn't enough time in the day to fully satisfy my desire to know her better. I want to journey, explore, and live abundantly with her. I live to experience her smiles and laughs (the dimples never get old), and I want to hold her when she cries. I want to take her hand and go to places we've never been. I want to please her in every way. I pray I will have many more years to share life with her. I can't get enough! Moreover, I have this sneaking suspicion the better I get to know her, the deeper our love will grow.

My relationship with my Heavenly Father is much the same, only deeper. This life will never quench my thirsting for more of Him. There is not enough time in the day to revel in His presence. There is not enough breath in my lungs to praise His Name! There is not enough time for me to read and comprehend all there is to learn about His character and nature, as it is revealed in the Scriptures.

We have defined abundant life as knowing God intimately. The question could then be raised, "How do you know God?" It is a very logical question. I recently was talking to a mom about her daughter's need for abundant life. The daughter was just experiencing "life" at the present time. Once the mom realized what Jesus defined as abundant life in John 17, she realized this was exactly what her daughter was longing for. That mom looked at me and said with a sense of urgency, "How then does my daughter get to know God that way?"

Where do you begin in this quest? Honestly, you must begin at salvation. If you have never invited God into your life by accepting His free gift of grace, you need to start there. There will be no relationship with God until you do this. As Paul writes in Ephesians, "You are dead in your transgressions and sins." You need the life-changing power of God. You need to be made alive by accepting God's free gift of grace through faith in His Son, Jesus Christ. It will change your life in remarkable ways!

From that point, knowing God intimately is much the same as knowing your spouse, brother, sister, parent, or friend. You do this by developing a relationship with Him. How do you develop a relationship with God? It's simple. You know the answer to this because you have built relationships with many people in your lifetime. It is really one word—**time**. You spend time with Him. The more you journey with Him, the deeper your relationship will go. The more you experience God, the more intense your love for Him will be.

There are three building blocks that will develop a relationship with God and help you really know God, not just know about Him. These three building blocks are so basic, you will probably be thinking, "Jamie, why are you writing a book about this? I learned this in Junior Church." Well, you probably did. But I want to look at these three elementary truths through different lenses. A fresh perspective is always helpful.

Building Block #1 – Read the Word

*"Your word, O Lord, is eternal; it stands firm in the heavens... How sweet are your words to my taste, sweeter than honey to my mouth!" – **Psalm 119***

What a treasure we have in the written Word of God. It is vitally important in this journey of knowing God intimately to remember the Bible reveals God to us. Guys, don't you wish that special girl you are pursuing would write you a letter explaining herself? What makes her laugh? What was her past like? What type of guy is she looking for? The Bible is our personal love letter, written by God, to reveal to us His person and His relationship with us as our Father. He tells us in this letter how He pursued us with His love, and this pursuit led to the death of His only Son, Jesus. He tells us we are significant because we are His children.

If your time in the Word seems dry and unsatisfying, maybe it is because you view the Bible as a factbook about God rather than the redemptive story of His love. The Bible as a factbook allows you to know about God, while the Bible as a love letter allows you to know God. There is a huge difference. It is like the difference between watching a documentary about William Wallace or viewing *Braveheart*. The documentary fills your head with facts and interesting tidbits about Wallace and his fight for freedom.

Braveheart captures your heart and motivates you to **live** with "freedom."

So what are you reading—factbook or love letter? Reading a factbook about God is something you check off your Christian to-do list, and this perspective will leave you incomplete and longing for something more. When you see the Bible for what it is—God's love letter to humanity—you read with a motivation fueled by love for your Heavenly Father. You can't get enough!

Building Block #2 – Prayer

"Pray continually." – I Thessalonians 5:17

Is this possible? Really? Is it possible to pray continually? Or as one version puts it, "pray without ceasing." Paul is telling the church of Thessalonica to never stop praying. You're thinking, "We all would have to become monks and move out of civilization to pray continually without stopping, right? Paul can't be serious. This is just one of those verses that we should strive for but know will never become a reality." Actually, to experience unceasing prayer, our perspective on prayer has to be altered. If prayer, in your thinking, consists only of bowing your head, closing your eyes, and praying through lists of requests, then there is no possible way to pray continually.

Now hear me clearly, prayer at times may be bowing your head, closing your eyes, and praying through lists, but that is not all prayer is. Prayer is so much more. I want to share with you a definition of prayer that completely revolutionized my prayer life. It comes from Dr. Jim King, Professor at Baptist Bible Seminary in Clarks Summit, Pennsylvania.

Prayer – *A conscious realization of a personal intimate relationship with a holy omnipotent God.*

It may take time to fully understand this definition. Go ahead and read it over again. Let the words begin to sink in, so your brain can digest it. Let's break it down.

Conscious realization

The relationship between God and a believer is marked by thought, will, design, and perception. It is a part of the thought process, a part of the worldview, and a part of every decision. The reality of the relationship is real, and the believer is fully aware of it each moment of the day. It means you are aware of God's presence in your life 24/7. So if you are at a coffee shop, at home, at work, at the mall, or at the gym, you understand God is present with you. You are in constant communion with God. The Most High is with you every moment of every day. Simply amazing!

Personal Intimate Relationship

Prayer is **personal**! Do you see God as a person? If you view God as this Being far away in heaven, you will struggle with your prayer life. God is a person. He has an intellect, emotions, and a will. You can talk to God just like you talk to your friends and neighbors. Prayer doesn't mean you have to use big, high-sounding theological words. We talk normally all day long. Then when we pray, we use this alternate vocabulary that we ourselves do not even understand. Jesus told his disciples in Matthew 6, *"And when you pray, do not keep on babbling like pagans, for they think they will be heard because of their many words."* Jesus wanted them and us to share our thoughts and feelings plainly in our own words.

Just today, I was really struggling, and I shared this with God. I shared with Him that I do not understand why it seems He is withholding something from my family. God already knew. Since He knows my thoughts, He didn't respond, "Jamie, I had no idea. Thank you for clueing me in." I was having those thoughts in my head, so why not share them with Him? I am so glad I could share those frustrations with Him. He didn't rebuke me. Rather, I sensed His presence and experienced His assistance, and my faith was rekindled. It can be the same for you. Tomorrow when you are walking to class or driving to work, just talk to God. Share everything with Him. Begin to share every moment of every day with Him.

Prayer is also **intimate**. It is a deep love relationship. In order for your prayer life to be intimate, you must share intimate things with God. My relationship with my wife Gretchen is the most intimate relationship I have with another human being. Why? Because we share deep, intimate things with one another. If I came home from work each day, ate dinner, had a casual conversation with Gretchen, turned on the TV, and didn't speak with her until I told her good night, I should not expect an intimate relationship when we go to bed. It is because we spend time together sharing our hearts, passions, struggles, hurts, joys, and desires that we experience a wonderful relationship.

If your prayer life consists of, "Thank you for this day," "Thank you for this food," "Bless us," "Be with us God," "Thank you for the beautiful weather," etc. then your relationship with God is shallow and not very fulfilling. You need to open up to God. Speak with Him in a personal, intimate way, as you would your closest friend.

Your prayer life is a constant realization of a personal, intimate **relationship**. We talked about this relationship in the previous chapter. The God of the Universe is your Father. Prayer flows from an understanding that you are a child of I AM. You are not a miserable, worm-like sinner but an heir of God, a child of the Most High. We can have boldness and confidence in His presence because of the work of Jesus on the cross. We come in His Name.

Characteristics of a personal intimate relationship include: a confidence that God is present with me, an assurance of God's acceptance, awareness that He is a person, a transparency that is honest, and a sweet fellowship.

Holy, Omnipotent God

Prayer causes a child of God to understand that God is the exalted One, perfect in goodness and righteousness, and alone worthy of complete devotion. The word "holy" means "sacred, or set apart." No one is like God. He is the only true, living God. It's important to remember that the relationship is between the creature, a believer, and the Creator, He who is absolute holiness and purity.

The word "omnipotent" means "all-powerful." When we pray, we are speaking with a God who is omnipotent and can do all that He desires for His children. When we commune with God, we are speaking to the only living God. He hears us and has the power to intervene in our lives. Isaiah 40 says this about our omnipotent God:

> "To whom will you compare me? Or who is my equal? Says the Holy One. Lift your eyes and look to the heavens: Who created all of these? He who brings out the starry host one by one, and calls them each by name.

Because of his great power and mighty strength, not one of them is missing…

The Lord is the everlasting God, the Creator of the ends of the earth. He will not grow tired or weary, and his understanding no one can fathom. He gives strength to the weary and increases the power of the weak."

We can pray without ceasing by simply making God a part of our consciousness and by communing with Him as a part of our life 24/7. The reality of His presence in our lives can be enjoyed, and His Spirit can direct our paths moment by moment. We do need specific times to be alone with our Heavenly Father to talk with Him about the thoughts and desires of our hearts much the same way it is necessary for a husband to have time with his wife and enjoy the emotional and spiritual intimacy of their marriage relationship. But, this alone is not the definition of prayer. Prayer is so much more. Do you see now that prayer is "a conscious realization of a personal, intimate relationship with a holy, omnipotent God?"

I think you see this now and want it... so where do you begin? Well, start right now. Put this book down immediately and simply begin talking to your Father. Don't worry about theological terms, God knows your thoughts. Don't worry about feelings of guilt or inadequacies. God took care of that through His Son on the cross. Come to your Father. He longs for you. He wants to commune with you.

"When he came to his senses, he said, 'How many of my father's hired men have food to spare, and here I am starving to death! I will set out and go back to my father and say to him: Father, I have sinned against heaven and against you. I am no longer worthy to be called your son; make me like one of your hired men.' So he got up and went to his father.

But while he was still a long way off, his father saw him and was filled with compassion for him; he ran to his son, threw his arms around him and kissed him." – **Luke 15:17-20**

Building Block #3 –
Be still & listen to God

I believe God desires to lead us each moment of every day, and He accomplishes this work through the power of the Holy Spirit. As a follower of Christ, you have the Holy Spirit indwelling you right now. He desires to commune with you and lead you. Jesus said about the Holy Spirit in John 14, *"All this I have spoken while still with you. But the Counselor, the Holy Spirit, whom the Father will send in my name, will teach you all things and will remind you of everything I have said to you."* How exciting is that? God indwells **you**. That is pretty mind-blowing in and of itself, but Jesus promised that the Holy Spirit will *"teach you all things."* He doesn't indwell you so He can hang out and be silent. He wants to help you learn and grow spiritually. He wants to take the words from Scripture and drop them into the grid of your life. He will guide and direct all your paths. I believe this happens in times of stillness.

Many people do not believe God communicates with them, but these people probably have never waited in stillness long enough to hear the Father's voice. It's not a voice that comes from the outside in, but one that emanates from inside of us. Take Jesus up on this. Ask God to have the Holy Spirit *"teach you all things."* Spend time in the Word. Saturate yourself with all God has communicated to you through the written Word, His love letter to you, and then get alone with God and simply tell him, "God, I'm here to listen to Your voice. Lead me. I long for You."

Just as reading the Word and praying take time to develop, listening to God is something that doesn't happen overnight. It will take a while to learn the discipline of being still. Our lives are overly cluttered. We have a hard time chiseling out fifteen minutes or so to read our Bibles and pray. But the rewards of being still are worth it, especially when the end result is hearing the voice of the Almighty.

Let me share a personal example of the Holy Spirit speaking from the inside. In August of 2004, we moved to the Twin Cities in Minnesota from northeast Pennsylvania. God had clearly communicated to us this was the next step in expanding Consumed Ministries to a global ministry. The only problem with this was that financially we were only at 10% of what we needed as a ministry, and my salary was part of that! Mix in the fact that we had established deep relationships with many people in Pennsylvania and that the college and singles group we led at our local church was at the brink of exploding, it wasn't an easy transition. We stepped out in faith and moved to Minnesota, believing God would provide for us since He had clearly communicated to us: "Go."

Two days after we arrived here, I became overwhelmed by all that was (or was not) happening and the reality that in six weeks our funds would be dried up. What were we going to do? Were my two little girls going to starve? As I sat in a coffee house reading my Bible, I sensed the Holy Spirit leading me to the

Gospels. I asked where, and He directed me to Matthew 17. This is what I read:

> *"Then the disciples came to Jesus in private and asked, "Why couldn't we drive it (demon) out?" He replied, "Because you have so little faith. I tell you the truth, if* **YOU** *have faith as small as a mustard seed,* **YOU** *can say to this mountain, 'Move from here to there' and it will move. Nothing will be impossible for* **YOU***."*

These words were not unfamiliar to me. We had just finished a study on faith with our college & singles group at the church we attended in Pennsylvania, and I had spoken with many friends regarding my family's "walk of faith." But that was then, this is now. I needed to let those truths sink in again. And in a moment of silence, the Holy Spirit communicated to me, "Jamie, I am going to use Consumed Ministries to move mountains." Oh, how I needed to hear that. Earlier Satan had been doing everything he could to get me to quit. As I type these words now (it's only two weeks later), we still are at 10% of our monthly support, and we haven't even scratched the surface for Consumed Ministries

Minnesota let alone Consumed Ministries International, but the Holy Spirit keeps reminding me throughout each day—"Mountains will be moved."

You too can experience the leading of God in your life. You can "know" God more intimately through His direct revelation to you each and every day. By reading the Word, praying, being still, and listening, you will begin to know God and uncover the abundant life He has for you. You will never be fully alive or satisfied here on earth until you have this deep relationship with your Father God. Go for it!

THE PYRAMID — THE GRID FOR ABUNDANT LIVING

It has been said many times in this book that the source of abundant life is the result of knowing the Father and having a deep, intimate, love relationship with Him. Nothing the world or religious institutions offer compares to this relationship because you were created to know God. When your relationship with God is deep, intimate, and passionate, other areas of your life will fall into place. Loving God should be at the top of the pyramid of your life. It is the filter through which all abundant living takes place. All other areas of life will flow out of this love for God. Let's explore!

IV.
LOVE GOD

In the book of Matthew, we are told that Jesus' adversaries desired to trap or trick Him. They often used deceptive questions to do so. The Pharisees and Herodians tried this tactic first, and then the Sadducees, but all failed miserably. It is rather funny to think these guys really thought they could trick the very Son of God. When the Pharisees found out that Jesus' answer had silenced the Sadducees, they pulled out what they considered to be their best option. They knew it was going to take their very best to out-wit this Rabbi Jesus. So the Pharisees sent an "expert in the law" to this intellectual duel. This guy was like the franchise player of team Pharisee. He was their top draft pick. He had studied the law since he was born, and he knew it backward and forward. He would have smacked that guy on Jeopardy who won like seventy matches in a row. If anyone was going to trap Jesus, this man was him.

He approached Jesus and said, "Teacher, which is the greatest commandment in the Law?" "Oh yeah, we have Him now," the Pharisee must have thought, which is why this guy was known as "the expert." The debate over the greatest commandment had been discussed by scribes for many years and the present religious leaders of the day argued this as well. All of them championed many of the laws as "the greatest." There were many laws to argue about too. Over the years, scribes had documented 613 commandments.

Jesus' response was very quick and to the point. "Love the Lord your God with all your heart and with all your soul and with all your mind. This is the first and greatest commandment. And the second is like it: Love your neighbor as yourself. All the Law and the Prophets hang on these two commandments." (reference) For the third time, Jesus had silenced the men competing in this intellectual battle. In Mark's account of this story, we are told that the "expert in the law" responded to Jesus' statement by telling Jesus His answer was correct. Jesus saw that the expert understood and said to him, "You are not far from the kingdom of God."

Love God, the first commandment Jesus spoke of, comes from Deuteronomy 6:4. It was known as the "Shema." This statement was recited every day by all orthodox Jews. Obviously they were very familiar with it. Possibly, they had become too familiar with the Shema. Perhaps they were simply repeating the words. It had become a routine religious practice. The second commandment quoted by Jesus concerning loving your neighbor is from Deuteronomy 19:18. The two statements completely sum up the Ten Commandments. The first four commandments deal with love for God, and the final six deal with love for mankind.

Here they are in case you forgot:

LOVE GOD

- *You shall have no other gods before me.*
- *You shall not make for yourself an idol in the form of anything in heaven above or on the earth beneath, or in the waters below.*
- *You shall not misuse the name of the Lord your God.*
- *You shall remember the Sabbath day by keeping it holy.*

LOVE MAN

- *You shall honor your father and your mother.*
- *You shall not murder.*
- *You shall not commit adultery.*
- *You shall not steal.*
- *You shall not give false testimony against your neighbor.*
- *You shall not covet your neighbor's belongings.*

Not only did Jesus' statements sum up the Ten Commandments but they also summarized the entire Old Testament. Loving God was the ultimate goal of His chosen people Israel. A pattern formed in the Old Testament is clear: when the Israelites loved and followed God, blessings were bestowed upon them; when they turned from their love of God and followed the evil practices of the pagan countries surrounding them, God judged them through droughts, war, or captivity.

We have done our best to make the Christian life more complicated than it needs to be. But maybe, just maybe, Jesus was on to something here. Maybe the most important thing in all of our lives is to simply love God. I'm thinking that since Jesus is the Son of God, I need to listen to what He said, and then put it into practice. The foundation for abundant living is loving God. Every other aspect of our lives flows out of this love for God. Think of the pyramid. If you love God, you will desire to love His other created beings. If you love God, you will want to remain personally holy. If you love God and love man, you will desire to use your talents and abilities for the glory of God's name and the edification of His children.

Heart, Soul, & Mind

Jesus said to love God with all that we are and have. First, He says to love God with all our "heart." Scripture attributes to the heart thoughts, affections, feelings, and reasoning. In other words, our motivation and passion come from the heart ... the soul. For an athlete, the "heart" is what pushes them to run sprints, train in the off season, dive on the floor, etc. It is what fuels their hunger to compete.

Before I started living abundantly, my loving God with all of my heart was not very evident. I knew how to love God with all of my mind. I memorized Scriptures, took notes while the pastor was preaching, and studied the Bible personally at home. Yet, I didn't love God with all of my affections and feelings. I didn't overflow with passion for my Father. The truths in my head only connected with my heart on rare occasions. Today, praise God, I'm a different person in this regard. My heart has been rescued, and I love God with every chamber of it. I can lift my hands to God in worship both corporately and personally with emotion and feelings of gratitude for all He has done for me. Now my outward actions are a natural response to what is happening inside... and it's real.

Second, we love God with all of our "soul." The soul refers to that immaterial part of a man. We love God with our "inner man." Our "soul" lives on for all eternity. It is interesting to note that Jesus doesn't mention anything about our physical bodies. He doesn't say, "Love God with all of your heart, 'physical body,' and mind." This vessel known as our body carries around our heart, soul, and mind, but it will perish. I am already feeling the effects of a body wearing down each time I run, lift weights, or play basketball. We love God with all of our soul—that part of us that will last for all of eternity encased in a new heavenly body.

Finally, Jesus says to love God with all of your "mind." The mind speaks of the intellect or understanding. We can love God with our mind by dwelling and meditating on Him all day long. In Ephesians 4, Paul is writing to believers when he says in vs. 17:

> *"So I tell you this, and insist on it in the Lord, that you must no longer live as the Gentiles do, in the futility of their thinking. They are darkened in their understanding (same word use in Matthew for mind) and separated from the life of God..."*

Paul says the Gentiles, or literally those outside of God, are "darkened in their minds." They do not know or love God in their understanding (same word as "mind" in Matthew 17). Because of this, they are separated from the life of God. Do you see how crucial the mind is? The mind is where Satan attacks. He uses human reasoning and logic to deter people from loving God in their minds. Many of our colleges are filled with intellectual darkness. People have reasoned God out of their lives by embracing scientific and human reasoning. Loving God with our mind defends us from the attack of the enemy.

To love God with all of our heart, soul, and mind is to love God with our entire being. To love God with all of our heart, soul, and mind is to love God with everything we have. We are to hold nothing back in this love relationship with our Heavenly Father.

Alive and free to love God

It is important to remember that we only have the ability to love God because He first loved us. In Ephesians 2, while writing to believers, Paul says, "You were (before they accepted God's gift of salvation) dead in your transgressions and sins." In my lifetime, I have been to my fair share of funerals. One thing I have never seen at a funeral is the person in the casket doing any kind of activity. They are not greeting people as they come into the church. They do not sing a song or preach the sermon. They can't. They are dead. Their life is gone, so they are incapable of doing anything. In order for them to take part in any of the activities, they would have to be brought back to life.

When Paul says "you were dead," he is speaking of spiritual deadness. He is telling the saints of Ephesus that before they knew Christ as their Savior, they were incapable of doing any spiritual activity. It was impossible, therefore, for them to love God. It was impossible because they were spiritually dead.

However, read on. Read verse four, which says, "But because of His great love for us, God, who is rich in mercy, made us alive with Christ even when we were dead in transgressions." We have the ability to love God because He made us alive, and Paul tells us that the motivation or reason for His doing so was His love for us.

This truth will never, ever get old to me. I was dead and incapable of doing anything to save myself, but God said, "I'm going to breathe new life into Jamie Miller and make him My son." I can love God because He loved me first. I was so undeserving. As a matter of fact, the only thing I deserved was death and separation from God. But God chose to look beyond my guilt and the filth of my sin and put His holy lips on mine and breathe life into my soul. He forgave every past sin I had committed and every one I will commit in the future. He welcomed me into His family and said, "I, the Almighty, Sovereign God, am here for you to know." Incredible!

Oneness with God

At the core of love is a desire for oneness or community. That is why the ultimate manifestation of love between humans is a sexual union between a husband and a wife. This is where two become one, and complete oneness is experienced.

Each of us has a longing in our souls to be connected with God and have a oneness or community with Him. Augustine prayed, "Thou has created us for thyself, and our hearts are restless until they rest in thee." We can never experience ultimate love until we experience community with God. That is why God's love for us is so amazing. Our sins separated us from God, yet He took the iniative and made oneness possible through the death of His only Son.

> *"God made him who had no sin to be sin for us, so that in Him we might become the righteousness of God."* – *2 Corinthians 5:21*

> *"But God demonstrates His own love for us in this: While we were still sinners, Christ died for us."* – *Romans 5:8*

> *"For God so loved the world that He gave His one and only Son, that whoever believes in Him shall not perish but have eternal life."* – *John 3:16*

An Example of Oneness

In the Old Testament, we find a patriarch who demonstrated a oneness with God evidenced by communion with Him. Genesis 5 contains one of those dreaded genealogies. I know genealogies are not the passages of

Scripture you turn to when you desire to revive your alone time with God. At best you skim over them, but more than likely you just completely skip them. In this genealogy, there are four amazing verses which speak of oneness with God. The first 20 verses are pure genealogy plugging along as usual. So and so lived so many years, he had a son, he lived some more years, and he died. On and on it went for generation after generation. He lived, he died. He lived, he died. But then we come to Enoch...

> *"When Enoch had lived 65 years, he became the father of Methuselah. And after he became the father of Methuselah, Enoch walked with God 300 years and had other sons and daughters. Enoch walked with God; then he was no more, because God took him away."*

Everybody else in this chapter lived and died, but Enoch walked and then was taken away. Talk about a contrast. Enoch understood abundant life thousands of years before Christ uttered the words in John 10. Enoch walked with God. He knew God. He journeyed with God every moment of every day. Because he was so close to God, God decided to "take him away" in this walk. Enoch understood what loving God was all about. He knew loving God is about experiencing oneness with the Almighty.

Let's parallel this passage in Genesis with Hebrews 11. Hebrews 11 is known as the hall of faith. Many giants of the faith such as Noah, Abraham, Isaac, and Moses are listed in this chapter. The second person mentioned is our man Enoch. Read what the author writes about Enoch:

> "By faith Enoch was taken from this life, so that he did not experience death; he could not be found, because God had taken him away. For before he was taken, he was commended as one who pleased God."

Enoch was commended as one who pleased God. What's the point? Well, we are told in Genesis that Enoch walked with God. Therefore, we can draw the conclusion that walking with God pleases Him. When we love God intimately and passionately pursue him manifesting a oneness with Him, God is pleased. The word "pleased" literally means "to be well, pleasing, to give satisfaction, make content."

Let me illustrate this for you. I have two beautiful daughters. Tori, my oldest, is four going on 17, and Isabelle is two. I know I am more than likely a bit biased; however, I think they are the cutest little girls in the entire world. Each day when I come home from work, both of them will run out to the car yelling excitedly, "Daddy, daddy!" I embrace them, and this feeling of contentment and satisfaction comes over me. At that moment, I am completely satisfied. After being away from them all day at work, just being with them gives me pleasure. Nothing else can begin to compare to that satisfaction.

Isn't is incredible then to think that God is completely satisfied and content when we simply walk with Him? When we love Him with all of our heart, soul, and mind, God is pleased. He is content. Nothing brings Him greater glory, honor, and pleasure than when we are fully alive by simply loving Him with all of our being. We can satisfy the Creator of the world through the oneness and communion we have with Him. Enoch figured this out and got his name listed along with some pretty stellar company in Hebrews 11.

I don't know where this chapter leaves you. It may be best right now to think of your life. What is at the top of your "pyramid"? Does life seem complicated and confusing? It doesn't have to be. Before you go on to the next chapter, take the necessary time to be still before the Lord. Let Scripture sink into your heart, soul, and mind. If you are one with the Father, your greatest duty is to love Him with your entire being by simply walking with Him every moment of every day.

V.
LOVE MAN

Friday, September 27, 2004, was quite possibly the hardest night of my life. Gretchen, my close friend Danny, his girlfriend Heather (they are married now), and I went to New York City for the day. I cannot remember when Danny and I were not friends. We grew up two doors apart in a subdivision of Columbus, OH. We both had three sisters and no brothers so, needless to say, we related well and formed a bond of brotherhood. We experienced much together growing up in Riverbend. We attended summer camps and played basketball, kickball, and football.

Danny and Heather came to visit us in Pennsylvania, but since Danny had never been to New York, we headed into the city to experience Manhattan and to catch a double-header between the Mets and the Atlanta Braves at Shea Stadium. It was great because Danny is a big time Braves fan. The games were very enjoyable, and it wasn't every day that I got the chance to sit down for four hours next to Danny taking in a baseball game and talking about old times, current events, and future dreams.

However, this enjoyable evening took a severe, life threatening turn. On the way back from Queens to Manhattan, we needed to switch trains. Unfortunately, Danny was struck in the head by the oncoming train. As he laid there, I had no idea what to do. I was paralyzed in fear. Gretchen grabbed me and said, "Do something." I immediately ran up the stairs looking for a police officer while begging God to spare Danny's life.

While I was gone, Danny laid there on the ground motionless and unconscious. It was about ten at night, and the station was still congested with commuters. Some were horrified by the event and just stood there watching. While others continued on their way not really bothered by what had just transpired. Heather was obviously a wreck, and Gretchen had no idea what to do. I was still running around upstairs looking for anyone in a uniform when out of nowhere a woman, who was a doctor at a nearby hospital, came over and checked all of Danny's vital signs. She held Danny's head still while he moved around in pain and anguish. She gave insight and direction to the EMTs when they arrived, and she worked with them to care for Danny. Looking back, we all know her expertise was key in keeping Danny alive. The police, EMTs, and staff at the nearby hospital also did a wonderful job of attending to Danny's needs. He is alive now, but we had six or seven scary days in the Intensive Care Unit as his life hung in the balance.

The doctor in the subway station serves to remind me of a person who puts into practice the second slot of the pyramid—"Love Man" or as the Bible says, "Love your neighbor." Hundreds of civilians in the station that night saw what happened to Danny, but only one (outside of the public servants, such as the police) did something about it. Her compassion for Danny motivated her and caused her to take action. That is what loving your neighbor means—Being filled with compassion and then acting on it.

As we continue to journey down the pyramid, we need to remember the principle of keeping it simple. Life doesn't have to be complex. If we love God, other things will fall into place. That is never more true than when we talk about loving others. If you love God, the second greatest commandment of loving your neighbor follows naturally. Usually, if someone is having a problem loving a neighbor, something is off in his love relationship with God. So I will say it once more, keep "Love God" at the top of your pyramid.

Jesus said in Matthew 22:39, *"And the second is like it: 'Love your neighbor as yourself'."* This prompts two questions which will be addressed in this chapter. First, *who is your neighbor?* Second, *how do you love your neighbor?*

The Good Samaritan

> *"A man was going down from Jerusalem to Jericho, when he fell into the hands of robbers. They stripped him of his clothes, beat him and went away, leaving him half dead. A priest happened to be going down the same road, and when he saw the man, he passed by on the other side. So too, a Levite, when he came to the place and saw him, passed by on the other side. But a Samaritan, as he traveled, came to where the man was; and when he saw him, he took pity on him. He went to him and bandaged his wounds, pouring on oil and wine. Then he put the man on his own donkey, took him to an inn and took care of him. The next day he took out two silver coins and gave them to the innkeeper. 'Look after him,' he said, 'and when I return, I will reimburse you for any extra expense you may have.'"* – Luke 10:30-35

This familiar story will greatly aid us as we seek to answer the two questions: *"Who is my neighbor,"* and *"How do I love my neigh-*

bor?" The story was told by Jesus in response to a question posed to Him. Let's back up in the text and see what transpired.

> *"On one occasion an expert in the law stood up to test Jesus. 'Teacher,' he asked, 'what must I do to inherit eternal life?' 'What is written in the law?' he replied. 'How do you read it?' He answered: 'Love the Lord your God with all your heart and with all your soul and with all your strength and with all you mind,' and 'Love your neighbor as yourself.' 'You have answered correctly,' Jesus replied. 'Do this and you will live'."* – Luke 10:25-28

Once again an expert in the law desired to trap Jesus. It was a legitimate question, but it came from wrong motives. Jesus pointed the man back to the law. He did this not because the law saves us but because the law shows us that we have a need for salvation. The law serves to convict sinners, helping them see their need of conversion. Jesus turned the tables on the expert. The expert sought to trap Jesus, but he ended up in the trap. The expert, knowing he was ensnared, should have pleaded with God for mercy right then and there. He knew he had not kept the complete law. But rather than acknowledging his sin, he tried to justify himself by making excuses. Read what Luke goes on to say:

> *"But he (expert) wanted to justify himself, so he asked Jesus, 'and who is my neighbor?'"* – Luke 10:29

As was Jesus' custom when a teaching moment evolved, first He told a story and then directed questions to the individual seeking wisdom rather than simply answering the question directly. The story of the Good Samaritan is one of the most familiar in the Gospels, and it serves as a guide for how to love our neighbors. Let's dig into it.

The distance between Jerusalem and Jericho is approximately 17 miles and has a descent from approximately 2,500 feet above sea level to 800 feet above sea level. The road was located in rocky, desert country, providing many places for robbers to attack defenseless travelers. The guy in the story obviously did not have a great day. He was stripped, beaten, and abandoned. Luke tells us that he was left half dead. I don't think any percentage of dead is a good thing. So if this guy was fifty percent dead, I'd say that was pretty bad, wouldn't you?

But wait, Luke tells us that *"a priest happened to be going down the same road."* If anyone would stop and help a guy that had been robbed and left naked and half-dead, surely it would be a priest. A priest was someone expected to love others. If this story took place in 2004, the priest would be a member of the clergy. Wouldn't you think a priest, pastor, or bishop would stop and help a man he saw lying in the middle of the road who was beaten, naked, and half-dead? Well, we know that this priest didn't. Not only did he not help, but Luke tells us that he *"passed by on the other side."* He totally avoided the guy.

Don't fret though, Luke goes on to tell us that a Levite also came to this place and saw the destitute man. Levites were descendants of Levi whom God had appointed to assist the priests in the temple. They would be like the deacons of today. Surely a Levite would stop and help this poor man in need. Not the case! Luke tells us that he too *"passed by on the other side."*

How could this be? How could a priest and a Levite both pass by this man without even checking to see if he is alive? I mean, they totally went out of their way to avoid him. They went to the other side of the road and slithered past. But before we completely condemn them, we should take a step back and inspect ourselves. Haven't we all passed by people in need? If the truth could be known, we probably used the same excuses that went through the minds of the priest and the Levite.

Excuse #1 – I have been so busy serving God all day today; I really need to get home.

Excuse #2 – Maybe the robbers are using this man as a trap. They probably are still lurking around here. I'd better get home.

Excuse #3 – This is a pretty busy road. Someone else will come along and help him.

Who knows what they were thinking. I know I have used those excuses to avoid giving assistance. I put myself and my agenda ahead of people in need rather than "loving my neighbor as myself."

But the story does not end here. The half dead man didn't become a hundred percent dead, because the most unlikely hero comes by to save the day. Samaritans and Jews were not fond of each other and they practiced open hostility towards one another. Point blank, they hated each other. They hated each other more than Ohio State hates Michigan. That, my friends, is severe hatred. By using a Samaritan as the hero, Jesus disarmed the Jews. The priest and Levite who were both Jews did not help a fellow Jew, but a Samaritan assisted a Jew? If anyone was going to just walk by on the other side of the road, you'd expect it to be the Samaritan. Actually, you might expect the Samaritan to not only ignore the Jew but to check for any money the robbers might have missed before. But that was not the case here.

Notice instead the major sacrifices the Samaritan made in order to help. The first thing we are told is that the Samaritan "took pity on him." Another version tells us that he *"felt compassion"* for the man. Literally, this expression means *"to have the bowels yearn."* The Samaritan truly hurt for this man in need, and since he was moved with compassion, he desired to help him.

Remember true sympathy or compassion prompts action. The Samaritan didn't say, "Oh that poor guy. I hope somebody helps him. I'll pray for him as I continue on my way." No, we are told the Samaritan *"bandaged his wounds, pouring on oil and wine."* He addressed the immediate needs of the man. He then took him to an inn and gave the innkeeper *"two silver coins"* or *"two denarii."* This would be around two day's wages and would keep someone in an inn for about two months. The Samaritan gave up two days wages to a complete stranger. He then said, *"And when I return…"* You mean he was coming back? Doesn't it seem he had already done enough? He had taken time out of his day to help the man physically and had provided more than enough money to insure proper care. Was he now saying he'd come back to check on the man and pay any other incurred expenses? Yes, that's what he was saying... and I'd say this Samaritan went above and beyond what a Samaritan would be expected to do for a Jew... or what most people would ever consider doing!

Who is my neighbor?

When Jesus finished the story, He asked the expert this question:

> *"Which of these three do you think was a neighbor to the man who fell into the hand of robbers?"*
> – Luke 10:36

Don't you just love Jesus? He completely turned the tables on the expert. The expert wanted to know *"Who is my neighbor?"* When he asked this question, he was trying to avoid the issue of assisting people in need. But when the story was told, Jesus asks the bigger question, *"To whom can I be a neighbor?"* This question has nothing to do with location, race, or relationship. Telling this story and asking the question allowed Jesus to explain to the expert just who the neighbor is. The neighbor is simply **anyone in need**.

And there are many people in need! Every where you look, people are in need. There are physical, emotional, and spiritual needs in every part of the globe. You can be in your dorm room, in your apartment complex, at your job, at the gym, at a coffee house, in your car, on vacation, or anywhere else, and you can be sure there will be people in need around you. All we need to do is open our eyes and discover the "neighbors" all around us.

It's amazing to think that God has placed you exactly where He wants you at this present time, so you can be a neighbor to the people in your sphere of influence who are in need. It isn't an accident or coincidence that you are working where you are. Your coworkers, fellow students, next-door neighbors, friends—

these people have needs! These needs will only be met by God's love flowing through you, His child. No, it is not mere chance that you presently live in your dorm room or neighborhood because there are people on your floor or on your block that have needs only the love of God can meet. It is not by mere chance that you are taking the classes you are this semester, because in your lab or in your classroom there are people that have needs only the love of God can meet. That love that can come through you. You have a divine appointment to be a neighbor to someone today!

How do I love my neighbors?

The question we need to ask ourselves is this: Do I look at my "neighbors" and have compassion as the Samaritan did? Do my bowels yearn when I see someone in need? Do I look at them through the eyes of Jesus and become so moved with compassion that I am prompted to action. We love our neighbors by meeting their needs. We do not just talk about assisting our neighbors, we *assist* our neighbors.

Many groups talk about "poverty," "feeding the hungry," "job opportunities," and "reaching their communities with the Gospel," but they do nothing about it. They never personally meet the needs of people. The expert was like this. Warren Wiersbe says this in his commentary about the expert, "He wanted to make the issue somewhat complex and philosophical, but Jesus moved it from duty to love, from debating to doing."

Jesus posed the question to the expert: "Who was the neighbor?" The expert replied, *"The one who had mercy on him."* Jesus then responds to the expert, *"Go and do likewise."* Christ gives us the same challenge. *"Go and do likewise."* Be a neighbor to someone today. Don't just plan, discuss, and strategize. Get out there and do something. Be a neighbor to the sick, tired, weary, and lost by meeting their needs. Feed the hungry, clothe the naked, and proclaim the Good News to the spiritually lost and blind.

The Ultimate Neighbor

Jesus is the ultimate example of being a neighbor. He saw many needs while He was on earth, and He saw the needs through the eyes of compassion.

> *"When he saw the crowds, he had compassion on them, because they were harassed and helpless, like sheep without a shepherd." – Matthew 9:36*

> *"When Jesus landed and saw a large crowd, he had compassion on them…" – Matthew 14:14*

> *"Jesus called his disciples to him and said, 'I have compassion for these people; they have already been with me three days and have nothing to eat.'" – Matthew 15:32*

> *"Jesus had compassion on them…" – Matthew 20:34*

The compassion Jesus felt for people prompted Him to act. He healed the lame, blind, and leprous. He fed the hungry five thousand after a long day of teaching. He met both the physical and spiritual needs of those with whom He came in contact.

But none of these actions compare to the ultimate sacrifice of the cross. We were people in need. Because of our sin, we deserved nothing except eternal separation from God. But Jesus saw our need, had compassion on us, stepped in to take our place as the needed perfect sacrifice, and took upon Himself our sins. He acted on our behalf, so we could live abundantly forever.

"He is the atoning sacrifice for our sins, and not only for our sins, but also for the sins of the whole world." – I John 2:2

"Greater love has no one than this, that he lay down his life for his friends." – John 15:13

"But God demonstrates his own love for us in this: While we were still sinners, Christ died for us." – Romans 5:8

"But because of his great love for us, God, who is rich in mercy, made us alive with Christ even when we were dead in transgressions." – Ephesians 2:4-5

Jesus was beaten, cursed, and spit upon to meet our need of atonement. He went the distance for us. He was the ultimate neighbor.

When loving God is at the top of your pyramid, you will come to understand the great sacrifice that was made so you could become a child of God. As you become conformed to the image of Jesus Christ, you will begin to see this world as a world full of people in need. Your eyes will take on a spiritual focus. You will be prompted to love others, because you will understand the God of the universe loved you first. Don't just sit there. Get out there, and be a neighbor to someone today!

CHAPTER FIVE

VI.
PERSONAL HOLINESS

When I went to college, I left behind my family and friends and traveled five hundred miles away from Columbus, OH, to northeast Pennsylvania. I never thought I would develop relationships at school like I had with my family and friends in Columbus.

But I was wrong. I developed life-long friendships while at college. Many of these friendships continue on today despite the miles that now separate us. We were there for each other through some very difficult moments and stood as witnesses at each others' weddings. At college, I was also welcomed into a new type of family. It was a "basketball family." I played on the basketball team all four years, and six of us were together all four years and became pretty tight. The basketball team was much more than 12-15 guys playing basketball guided by a coaching staff. We were a family! There is nothing like a five month season filled with hard practices, road trips, parties, buffalo wings, defeats, and victories to build relationships.

Our coach, Mike Show, made it quite clear to us that being a member of the basketball team also meant being a part of a close-knit family. We knew Coach Show loved us. To him, our relationship was much more than coach and player. He opened his home to us. My fellow teammates and I spent countless hours at his home watching football, basketball, and boxing. Many seasons our schedules would not allow us to get home for Thanksgiving or New Year's Day. Not a problem for the basketball family; we spent it together. I even spent two Thanksgiving meals with Coach Show and his family while I was in college.

Coach loved his players. He put our needs ahead of his. Let me give just one example of many. My senior year we competed in our National Tournament in Oklahoma City. We were away from the college from Tuesday morning until Sunday afternoon. When we returned, I tried to start my truck and realized I had some problems with the engine. I had no clue what was wrong, (I still would not know) so I called Coach Show. He is a "jack-of-all-trades" kind of guy. Poor Coach Show had been away from his wife and son for six days. He gets home for about two hours and I call and ask if he can help me with my truck. Now I realize what an idiot I was, but at the time, Coach Show said nothing. He just told me to bring the truck over, so he could help me figure out what was wrong. He took care of the problem, and he will never know how much that meant to me.

Coach Show had his own set of rules for the team. Some of these rules had nothing to do with basketball. They were just his preferences and because he was the coach, he expected us to abide by them. A few examples: we were not allowed to wear a hat inside the building, we had to tuck in our practice jerseys, we were required to wear socks with our sandals during summer basketball camps, and we were to keep our headphones in our gym bags when we left the bus.

Honestly, I thought some of those rules were pretty silly. Come on Coach, tube socks with sandals? This was not exactly cutting edge style back then. But you know what? We didn't care. We loved coach, so we obeyed. Period. No questions asked. It didn't matter to us what he required. We were willing to do anything he asked, because we loved him. We loved him, because we knew he loved us.

"If you love me, you will obey what I command."

Love should be the motivation for our obedience. In John 14, Jesus says this three times:

"If you love me, you will obey what I command."
— Vs. 15

"Whoever has my commands and obeys them, he is the one who loves me." — Vs. 21

"If anyone loves me, he will obey my teaching."
— Vs. 23

It is quite simple, isn't it? Elementary almost. If you truly love God, you will obey what He commands. Just as my team was obedient to Coach Show because of our love for him, we who are God's children should obey our Heavenly Father because we love Him. Many churches have made this simple truth much too complicated. They have become like the Pharisees of Jesus' day. The Pharisees took pride in memorizing all 613 of the commands given in the Old Testament, which is truly a remarkable accomplishment. But they didn't just desire to memorize these commands, they also strove to obey them. To help them obey these commands, they concocted many religious rules, man-made guidelines that altered the originals to make obedience easier.

We do the same thing today by constructing religious "do's and don'ts." I know churches where pastors preach against going to a movie theatre. Movie theaters are considered in and of themselves to be evil. However, these same pastors say nothing about renting DVD's at the local Blockbuster. According to this logic, a member of the church would be sinning if he went to see The Passion at the theatre, but he could rent a movie filled with sex, nudity, and crude language and watch it in the privacy of his own home. In this instance, sin is the size of the screen and not the content that is filling the mind.

Churches can be very unsuccessful at trying to establish personal holiness through external, man-made regulations. "Don't drink, don't chew, don't go out with girls that do!" There are religious meetings happening all over the world where small groups of men and women get together to discuss their external actions. Picture five mature, adult saints of God sitting at a table. Jim, the moderator, looks at Tim. "Tim, have you had any impure thoughts this week?" "No," replies Tim. Jim continues, "Did you steal from your company by not giving a hundred percent every hour of every day?" "No," Tim answers once again. Many other questions like this follow. Then Jim asks his final question, "Tim, did you lie about anything you answered today?" "No," Tim says calmly.

Now it's Frank's turn. "Before I answer any questions, guys, I have to admit something to you. This week I struggled again and looked at an inappropriate magazine." The other four guys look at Frank with disgust on their faces. "How could you, Frank?" Jim asks. "You know the Bible says 'Anyone who looks at a woman lustfully has already committed adultery with her in his heart.' You committed adultery, Frank! You must confess this immediately."

I know these groups meet with good intentions. They exist so Christians can help each other keep Scriptural commands and become more like Jesus. I have been involved in men's small groups that aided me in my walk with Christ. But external, man-made practices alone will not produce personal holiness. Churches that have stopped focusing simply on outward actions and have begun encouraging saints to be lovers of God are producing Christians who obey God's commands because they love Him. That love creates a desire to obey.

I want to be involved in a Christian community where saints talk about the immense love of God for us, His children. I want to win the hearts of my brothers and sisters in Christ by continually reminding them they are saints in the eyes of the King and are no longer bound by the chains of sin. They are truly free to know, love, and serve God. This inward, true love for God will produce outward obedience. Jesus said so!

What are His Commands?

Seems like an important question, right? If Jesus asks us to keep His commands, we need to know what they are. As I did in previous chapters, let me quote Jesus' response to the expert's question, "Which is the greatest command?"

> *"'Love the Lord your God with all your heart and with all your soul and with all your mind.' This is the first and greatest commandment. And the second is like it: 'Love your neighbor as yourself.' All the Law and the Prophets hang on these two commandments." –* Matthew 22:37-40

"Personal Holiness" is placed under "Love God" and "Love your Neighbor" on the pyramid, because it follows them in a natural progression. If we love God, we will love our neighbors. If we love God, we will desire to keep His commands and be personally holy. What are His commands? Just look at the pyramid. They are summed up for you, "Love God" and "Love

Man." It almost seems too easy. Maybe, just maybe, God desired it to be that easy. Maybe we have made things more complicated than they need to be.

The Reward

We have been conditioned to believe good behavior merits rewards. As a young student, I despised English. I do not think I really learned the rules for participles until I took Greek in college. I had to learn Greek before I could understand English. My mom, out of desperation when I was little, tried to motivate me in my study of the English language by promising lunch at the Pizza Hut buffet if I received a "B" or higher on my report card. Food has always been a motivational incentive for me. I will do almost anything for pizza, steak, or anything sweet. I remember a few lunches when I consumed slice after slice of pepperoni, supreme, and sausage pizza as a reward for my countless hours in the books (countless might be an exaggeration).

In John 14, Jesus lists rewards for those whose love for God is evidenced by their obedience to His commands:

> *"Whoever has my commands and obeys them, he is the one who loves me. He who loves me will be loved by my Father, and I too will love him and show myself to him." – John 14:21*

> *"If anyone loves me, he will obey my teaching. My Father will love him, and we will come to him and make our home with him." – John 14:23*

Jesus is not teaching a works-based faith but that true faith produces obedience. We are told that both the Father and the Son will love him or her who loves Him. The Father and Son's love cannot be separated. Jesus does not stop with just love. He also says He will show himself to those that love Him, and He and the Father will make their home in those that love Him. Another translation uses "abode" for "make our home." This word literally means "to remain or dwell." The word is tied to mansions earlier in John 14.

> *"When the sinner trusts Christ, he is born again and the Spirit immediately enters his body and bears witness that he is a child of God. The Spirit is resident and will not depart. But as the believer yields to the Father, loves the Word, prays, and obeys, there is a deeper relationship with the Father, Son, and Spirit. Salvation means we are going to heaven, but submission means that heaven comes to us" (Warren Wiersbe, The Bible Exposition Commentary 353).*

Because we love God, He "made His home" in our hearts. Paul understood this truth. His prayer for the saints at Ephesus: "I pray that out of his glorious riches he may strengthen you with power through his Spirit in your inner being, so that Christ may dwell in your hearts through faith." The God of the Universe is right at home in the hearts of those who love Him. I can't even begin to comprehend this, but Scripture tells me it is true. What a reward!

Once again, the Perfect Example

"...but the world must learn that I love the Father and that I do exactly what my Father has commanded me."
— John 14:31

Jesus is always the ultimate example for us. That is why we are called Christians. Our lives should be a reflection of Christ. We are to be imitators of the ultimate example – Jesus. Jesus taught His disciples about love and obedience in John 14. He finished His teaching on love by explaining His obedience to His Father. He does exactly what His Father commands Him to do. He does so because He loves His Father.

What is unbelievable about these words is the context in which Jesus speaks them. This conversation between Jesus and His disciples took place either in the upper room or as they made their way to the Garden of Gethsemane. In either situation, Jesus is just hours away from fulfilling His purpose for coming to earth as a man, which was to obey His

Father by becoming the perfect atonement for the sins of mankind. He was willing to be "obedient to death, even death on a cross."

Is it really necessary to say that this was not an easy command to obey? He was going to be "obedient to death, even death on a cross." What prompted that degree of obedience? Jesus obeyed because of His love for the Father. Note that as Jesus prayed in the garden, He prayed so intensely that He sweat drops of blood that dripped from his forehead. Matthew tells us that "He fell with his face to the ground" as He prayed.

> *"My Father, if it is possible, may this cup be taken from me. Yet not as I will, but as you will." – Matthew 26:39*

> *"My Father, if it is not possible for this cup to be taken away unless I drink it, may your will be done." – Matthew 26:42*

The bottom line is that Jesus wanted a different way. Jesus wanted the payment of your sins and my sins to be completed without His body being ripped apart. But His prayer was, "not as I will, but as you will." Love was the great motivator. Christ came to give us abundant, overflowing life, but it came at a great cost. He knew this and yet was obedient to His Father because He loved Him.

Just as Christ loved His Father and displayed it by His obedience, we ought to love our Redeemer and King the same way. And Jesus says we will if we obey His commands to love God and love our neighbor.

VII.
FULFILL YOUR ROLE

We end our journey of the pyramid with a most exciting truth. We all have a role to play! You see, if you love God and man, you will want to fulfill your role for the glory of God and the edification of the body. It is a natural procession.

This aspect of the abundant life is very meaningful to all of us who are a part of the family of God because within us is an innate desire to be a part of something greater than ourselves. Life would be extremely boring if it consisted only of going to class, going to work, coming home, studying, hanging out, going to sleep, and repeating this pattern day after day. What is the adventure in that? True adventure is moving beyond the physical and doing something that matters in spiritual realms. It is amazing to think that God has equipped and designed each of us with particular passions, talents, and gifts to use for His eternal purposes. He desires to use us to further His kingdom, to rescue hearts, and to defeat the enemy. He desires to use us to edify and equip the body of Christ! Each role is vital. Without you playing your part, the entire body will suffer. Wait! You don't believe me? Let God's Word open your eyes.

Who designed you?

> *"For you created my inmost being; you knit me together in my mother's womb. I praise you because I am fearfully and wonderfully made; your works are wonderful, I know that full well." – Psalm 139:13-14*

I've often heard these verses used to convince someone that their physical looks are precious to God. I know they were quoted to me during my awkward junior high years. And that is one connotation of these verses. But it's more than merely the physical. God has designed you! He created you in your mother's womb. He made you the wonderful person you are. This includes not only your physical attributes but also your talents, gifts, and abilities. He gave you that amazing voice, ability to cook, athletic ability, intellectual capabilities, or servant's heart. God did that! This isn't something that happened by chance. He designed you! The Creator of the world designed you exactly the way He wanted to.

In the New Testament, we find more proof. God is in the business of giving spiritual gifts as well. We see this in I Corinthians 12:

"There are different kinds of gifts, but the same Spirit. There are different kinds of service, but the same Lord. There are different kinds of working, but the same God works all of them in all men."

"Now to each one the manifestation of the Spirit is given for the common good."

"To one there is given through the Spirit..."

"But in fact God has arranged the parts of the body, every one of them, just as he wanted them to be."

"...But God has combined the members of the body..."

"And in the church, God has appointed..."

Warren Wiersbe says this in The Bible Exposition Commentary,

"The source of the gift is God; the sphere for administering the gift is for God; and the energy to use the gift is from God."

God...God... God! God gave you the talents, gifts, and abilities He desired you to have. That is why you are special. You do not teach simply because teaching is in your genes. You teach because God made you a teacher. Allow that to sink in... God designed you. Take time right now to thank Him for all the abilities He has given you. He gave them to you, so you can have a part in His story!

Who does my role serve?

> *"Consequently, you (those that have been "made alive")*
> *are no longer foreigners and aliens, but fellow citizens*
> *with God's people and members of God's household..."*
> – *Ephesians 2:19*

When God made you alive, rescuing you from death, He placed you in His household. You became a member of the body of Christ. That is why your role is important! God chooses to use His body, the universal church, to accomplish His will on earth! Yes, I'll say it again... God desires to use you as a member of His body to carry out His mission on earth. If you do not fulfill your role, the body of Christ will suffer! That is why it is extremely important for you to know your role and then fulfill it. Let's talk more about the body.

There are some key truths about the body we can't overlook. First, we need to understand that the body is a unit made up of different parts.

"The body is not made up of one part but of many." –
I Corinthians 12:14

*"Now you are the body of Christ, and each one of you
is a part of it."* – *I Corinthians 12:27*

*"...so in Christ we who are many form one body, and
each member belongs to all the others."* – *Romans 12:5*

There are differences in the
parts of the body, yet we are all part of the same
unit. We are tied together through the blood of
Jesus Christ, which is why the physical body of a
human is such a wonderful example of the spiritual body of Christ. The human body has many
different parts. It has a head, nose, brain, heart,
liver, feet, ears, eyes, hands, elbows, fingers, etc.
All of these parts are different, but they are a
part of the same body. That is how it is in the
body of Christ. My brothers and sisters in Christ
are nothing like me ... and that's good! If all
members of the body were designed like Jamie
Miller, the body would not function very well. I

am uniquely designed by God to play a part in His Body. Rejoice in your uniqueness. There is no one else in the body like you.

Second, God arranges the parts of the body. We previously covered this, but it needs to be said again. This is an important truth about the body. By His choice, He made you a finger, elbow, or knee. That's the role you are to play. You can be confident of that, and you can rejoice in that.

Third, every member is vital to the life of the body.

> *"Now the body is not made up of one part but of many. If the foot should say, 'Because I am not a hand, I do not belong to the body,' it would not for that reason cease to be part of the body. And if the ear should say, 'Because I am not an eye, I do not belong to the body,' it would not for that reason cease to be part of the body. If the whole body were an eye, where would the sense of hearing be? If the whole body were an ear, where would the sense of smell be? But in fact God has arranged the parts in the body, every one of them, just as He wanted them to be. If they were all one part, where would the body be? As it is, there are many parts, but one body." – I Corinthians 12:14-20*

Paul says it better than I ever could. You have been designed to do something no one else in the body of Christ can do. If you do not bring that to the table, the body may not be able to "smell," "hear," or "see." I'll say it one more time, your role is vital.

Finally, if one member of the body does not use his or her gifts, the entire body suffers. Paul says in I Corinthians 12:26, "If one part suffers, every part suffers with it…" I'm sure you have stubbed your toe or burned your hand once or twice in your lifetime. It is amazing what happens to the entire body when one little part is affected. The whole body suffers with it. The performance of the body is hindered when just the smallest little part is harmed. That is why professional athletes miss games because of "turf toe" or shin splints. They cannot function a hundred percent with these seemingly minor injuries.

The same is true with the body of Christ. If you do not fulfill your role, the body does not function as smoothly as it should. It will suffer. You have something amazing to offer and if you choose to sit on the sidelines, we (the body of Christ) suffer because of it. Where would the body of Christ be if Billy Graham decided he couldn't preach? Or if John Eldredge, John Piper, or Erwin McManus said, "No one will read my books so I'm not going to write?" I would have suffered because these men have changed my life.

My life has also been changed by Keith Fluharty. What? You have never heard of him? Probably not. He was my high school Sunday School teacher and without him, I may never have learned to study the Bible on my own. I may never have chosen the college I did. That would mean I would have never married my wife Gretchen. I never would have met Dan Shearer and Eric Beavers, the guys who are on the Consumed Ministries staff with me. Most likely Consumed never would have been established, and if Consumed had never begun, possibly thousands of college students would not hear the message of abundant life. Without Keith Fluharty performing his role, the body of Christ would have suffered.

Sounds like the classic movie It's a Wonderful Life, doesn't it? George Bailey is contemplating suicide when good old Clarence shows him what the town would be like if he had never been born. George realizes the influence he has had on so many people and he begins to believe his life is important. He realizes he has had a "wonderful life." Admit it. You cry every time you hear his brother Harry say at the end, "George Bailey, the richest guy in town." Why do you cry? Because that movie helps you realize that your life is also important. You realize you desire to have a "wonderful life." You want a life that makes a difference.

As part of the body of Christ, your life has greater influence than George Bailey's had. Your role in the body has eternal influence, so never underestimate your influence. Never belittle the role God has asked you to play.

It is important...vitally, eternally important. God created you for it. There are members of the body that could be greatly harmed if you decide to sit it out.

What is my role?

By this point, you may agree with me. Or better said, maybe you agree with God's Word. You do have a role to play and that role is important. But now you might be asking, "I don't know my role. How do I find it? What are my gifts? "

"Delight yourself in the Lord and He will give you the desires of your heart." – Psalm 37:4

I believe this verse sums it all up for us. In a sense it connects the pyramid for us. It connects "Love God" with "Fulfill Your Role." The word "delight" means "to live or spend in enjoyment." So when "delighting" in God or loving God is at the top of your pyramid, God promises you that He will give you the desires of your heart. Did you catch the emphasis there? If you truly delight yourself in the Lord, you can trust your heart. Why? Because God put those desires in you. He put those passions in you. If God is your delight, chase after your dreams because they are the dreams God gave you. God in a sense is saying, "You are free to follow your desires my child. I put them in your heart." It is as John Eldredge put it in his book Journey of Desire:

> *"What if the Master's invitation was to do, like Hopkins, what is you? What if you were given the freedom (the permission) and the power (all the resources necessary) to do exactly what you were always meant to do? "*

I know of people that are chasing their dreams … and in truth, God's purpose for their lives. It's exciting to watch their journey. I have a friend named Mark whose passion is basketball. He loves the game and the satisfaction and enjoyment that teaching and coaching bring. Currently, he is an assistant coach at a small college, but he believes God will someday give him a head coaching position at the collegiate level. Right now, he is doing everything he can to prepare for that day. He is studying films, shaping his philosophy of the game, sending out his résumé, and trusting God's perfect timing of it all.

Or there is Judith. Judith has already received a lot of education. She has worked several jobs but has never been satisfied. Why? Because her life-long goal was to be a nurse, not just work a job that's uninteresting and unfulfilling to her. So she decided to go for it. She is immersed in her nursing education now, preparing for the day she will help people with their physical needs. She recently told me that she is completely happy. She is preparing for her dream. She also told me that when she is finished with her education, she would like to travel the country, working as a nurse at multiple hospitals. What an adventure!

Or this band Cofield. They are a group of friends that God put together to lead worship at a weekly outreach worship gathering for a community college in the Twin Cities. They love writing and playing music for people, so they decided to go for it. All of them are working other jobs to get by financially while performing for venues on nights and weekends. They long for the day when Cofield becomes their full-time job.

I could go on and on with stories like this ... stories of others in the body of Christ that are going for it. It inspires me to dream big dreams and follow my heart. I want to follow the passions God has given me. What about you?

What is my passion?

I think that's a relevant question. If you are going to first "delight yourself in the Lord" and then go for the desires in your heart, you had better know what those desires are... but how? How do you locate those desires? I want to share with you some questions I found from Mels Carbonell, Ph.D. and Steve Harbin in their pamphlet Discovering Your Divine Design.

These questions are taken from a section called the Passion Profile. I share them with you, not so you'll read through them with little thought but with a prayer that you'll take the time to think through them so the answers can give you real insight. If you do, these questions will help you understand the answer to the greater question, "What role does God want me to play in His body?"

What has been the most successful accomplishment in your life?

What activity or ministry generates your greatest emotional response?

What activity or ministry brought you your greatest disappointment or fear?

For what are you willing to take the highest risk?

If you could do anything for God, what would you do?

If someone were to mention your name to a group of associates or friends, what would they say you were really interested in or passionate about?

What conversation would keep you talking late into the night?

What issues do you feel strongly about?

More than likely there is a common thread throughout all of your answers. How do you know if this is not only your passion, but God's plan and purpose for your life? Pour out your heart to your Father. Ask Him to reveal to you what your passions are. He will do it if we ask! He will make things clear! Just trust Him. If He promises to give you "the desires of your heart," you can count on it happening.

James 4:14 describes your life as "a mist that appears for a little while and then vanishes." That's the bottom line. If you only have a mist, you better get every ounce of moisture out of it. Discover your passion and then go for it! Reach for the stars! Just try and dream dreams as big as God! He is a limitless, almighty, amazing God. He desires to use you to accomplish His will on earth. Amazing thought, isn't it?

"Now to him who is able to do immeasurably more than all we ask or imagine, according to his power that is at work within us, to him be glory in the church and in Christ Jesus throughout all generations, for ever and ever! Amen." – Ephesians 3:20-21

EPILOGUE

I went back to the Thirsty Conference in Alpharetta, GA, this past spring. Externally, the scene was similar to my first Thirsty experience. The worship leaders were using their gifts and talents to lead us to the throne, children of God were worshipping their Heavenly Father, music was cranking, and lights were moving. But internally, deep in my soul, things were drastically different. We were singing a line of a song that repeated "I'm alive" over and over again. "I'm alive, I'm alive, I'm alive, I'm alive"… it went on and on and on. As I stood there singing this line, my heart filled with gratitude and praise to God. I was indeed alive. I had discovered what the Holy Spirit had communicated to me two years earlier. I had discovered what the "more" was. It was abundant life.

Once I realized the "more" I was looking for was the abundant life found in knowing God in a deep, intimate, and relational way, my Christianity had meaning, purpose, adventure, and life. Everything I do now flows through that love relationship with God. It is the pyramid of my life. Praise God for opening my eyes!

Abundant living is available for you. Jesus came to give abundant life to you! Will you walk in it? Take Jesus up on His offer. An adventure is waiting for you. He is worth it!

The glory of God is man fully alive. — Saint Irenaeus

WANT MORE FROM
CONSUMED MINISTRIES?

Check us out on the web!

www.consumedministries.com

www.consumedministries.blogspot.com

Or...

Listen to our podcast...

We can be found on itunes!